Original title:
The Song of Spruce

Copyright © 2025 Creative Arts Management OÜ
All rights reserved.

Author: Nolan Kingsley
ISBN HARDBACK: 978-1-80567-227-2
ISBN PAPERBACK: 978-1-80567-526-6

Lullaby of the Woodlands

In a forest where the trees sway,
Odd critters dance and play all day.
A squirrel spins, wearing a hat,
Chasing shadows, where's the cat?

Frogs join in with a wild croak,
While rabbits giggle at every joke.
Twigs and branches start to clap,
In this woodland, there's no nap!

Voices of the Northern Sky

The owls hoot in silly tones,
Chasing echoes, they rattle bones.
A moose prances, quite absurd,
He thinks he's singing, but it's a blur.

Clouds drift by, they play peek-a-boo,
With playful winds that swirl and woo.
Stars twinkle, giggling with glee,
As night turns into a comedy spree.

Symphony of the Conifers

The pine cones drop, like popcorn afar,
A woodpecker's drum is the best rock star.
Trees sway, like they're at a prom,
With branches twirling, keep calm and carry on.

A chipmunk juggles acorns on high,
While the fox teaches dance to a shy fly.
Harmony reigns, in laughter we bask,
Nature's jest, is a colorful mask.

Rhythms in the Rustling Leaves

Rustling leaves make funny sounds,
The best orchestra, in these grounds.
A raccoon tap dances on a log,
While the crickets chirp, as they hog.

Each leaf whispers a cheeky tale,
Of squirrels stealing snacks without fail.
In every rustle, a quirky rhyme,
Nature's laughter, a twist of time.

Tales in the Twilight Canopy

Beneath the branches, muffled cheer,
The squirrels gather, full of beer.
They dance around with acorn hats,
While raccoons laugh at all the chats.

A woodpecker joins, tapping a beat,
The laughter grows with every repeat.
A hedgehog in shades starts to groove,
Cracking jokes, he's got the move.

Each creature's tale, a funny twist,
In twilight's glow, they can't resist.
With every giggle, shadows shift,
In the canopy, there's no grift.

Lyrics from the Knotted Roots

The roots conduct a silent band,
With twists and turns, they take a stand.
A rabbit hopped, then trip and fell,
He laughed, he rolled, 'It's just as well!'

The badger plays on muddy drums,
While tiny critters hum like bums.
A toad serenades, croaking quite rude,
With verses about his dinner food.

In knotted chaos, tunes arise,
With every note, the laughter flies.
These underground shows, they bring delight,
In burrows deep, beneath the light.

Brushstrokes of a Timbered Tale

With paintbrush tails, the mice create,
A masterpiece that can't wait.
They giggle as they splash the tree,
"Oh, what fun! Let's paint the bee!"

A bear wanders in smelling sweet,
Mistaking paint for honey treat.
He dips his paw, but oh, what mess!
Now he's a canvassed, fluffy mess.

In timbered art, each stroke absurd,
As owls watch on, and shake their head.
With every hue, the fun expands,
An artist's life is in the hands.

Epiphany Among the Resilient

A wise old tree whispers low,
"See the squirrels? They steal the show!"
The chipmunks nod, with cheeks so round,
Life's lessons learned from nutty ground.

Among the branches, tales unfold,
Of antics shared, of laughter bold.
A prancing fawn, with fashion flair,
Wears leaves for shoes, without a care.

In this world, where joy's the aim,
Resilience taught, but never lame.
With silly faces, and antics bright,
Life's woes dissolve, in pure delight.

Dreams of the Stillness

In the quiet woods, a squirrel pranced,
Wearing acorn hats, he took a chance.
He'd boast to friends with a nutty grin,
'This crown of snacks, let the feast begin!'

Amid the trees, a log rolled around,
With giggles of moss, they danced on the ground.
A party of ferns waved their leafy arms,
As the drowsy raccoon snored, a lullaby's charms.

Whimsy Beneath the Hemlocks

Beneath the hemlocks, a gnome spun in place,
With a twirl of his beard, he raved with grace.
He juggled some pine cones, a sight to behold,
While squirrels chimed in with tales to be told.

The shadows would shift, as the gnome let out laughs,
Leading the critters in patterned giraffes.
In nutty accord, they boogied and swayed,
A whimsical ball that the moon had displayed.

Sonnet of the Reaching Crown

Up high, the pine's lofty limbs do extend,
As a crow, in style, begins to descend.
He lands with a flair, on a branch all austere,
And caws out a tune that only he hears.

Beneath, a party of spiders would scheme,
To knit him a nest, what a curious dream!
With threads made of laughter, in sunbeams they twined,
Their webs sparkled light, and the crows were aligned.

Interludes of the Ancient Biota

The moss started gossiping near the old oak,
With secrets of youth, they tried not to choke.
'Did you see how the beetle just slipped on a leaf?'
They chuckled together, the grandfathers of mischief.

A snail told a tale with a custard-like flair,
Of the time he raced and lost in mid-air.
With laughter like rain, the forest held tight,
To the jests of the critters, from morning to night.

Murmurs of the Forest Elders

In the shade, old trees gossip,
About squirrels stealing their acorns,
They chuckle at the silly bear,
Who trips on roots, and that's no fair!

The owls debate in midnight hues,
While raccoons play cards with their shoes,
A fox in a hat shares a joke,
Laughter floats high, not a single yoke.

Beneath the boughs, the laughter flies,
With wind that tickles, oh how it sighs,
The pine cones laugh, they roll with glee,
What a jolly, leafy jubilee!

When the sun dips low, and shadows creep,
The forest hums, a song so deep,
A melody of mirth and play,
In nature's hall, they dance away.

Crescendo of the Wild Whispering Woods

In the woods where giggles bloom,
The critters plot a grand costume,
A bunny dons a dapper tie,
While ants march by, oh my, oh my!

Among the branches, a chipmunk prances,
Spreading news of all wild romances,
A hedgehog winks, a secret to keep,
Under the stars, they'll laugh and leap.

Squirrels juggle acorns with flair,
While owls hoot in the midnight air,
A raccoon steals snacks from the stash,
Chasing shadows with a sneaky dash.

As twilight fades, the jokes abound,
Echoes of laughter in every sound,
The woodland chorus sings out loud,
A jovial tune from the gathered crowd.

Whispers of Evergreen

Under the pines, a secret's shared,
With giggles spread, none are spared,
A deer slips in, with a wink and a nod,
While frogs jump in, feeling quite odd.

Branches sway to a cheeky beat,
As beetles tap dance with their tiny feet,
A woodpecker pecks in a silly style,
Causing the trees to grin all the while.

The moss softens every silly fall,
In this green realm, there's room for all,
Breezes carrying tales of fun,
Under the bright and glowing sun.

At dusk, the forest tells tales merry,
With whispers sweet, like a vision fairie,
A banquet of joy beneath the leaves,
Where laughter lingers, and magic weaves.

Melodies in the Canopy

In the treetops high, a songbird croons,
While chipmunks dance under glowing moons,
A playful gust stirs those branches wide,
Free-spirited sprites take joy in the ride.

Fiddling foxes sing in delight,
As fireflies flash, lighting up the night,
A bear joins in with a little jig,
The woodland choir swells, oh so big.

Rustling leaves add to the cheer,
With every note, the laughter near,
In the canopy where spirits gleam,
Life is but a whimsical dream.

When dawn arrives, the fun won't cease,
The forest revels in a capering peace,
For every tree has a tale to spin,
In this merry maze, we all fit in.

Whispers of the Evergreen

In the forest, trees do chat,
With secrets wrapped in fluffy sprat.
Squirrels steal the show with grace,
While birds hum tunes that quicken pace.

Pinecones giggle in the breeze,
As they tumble, bouncing—oh, what a tease!
Every rustle's a joke that's cracked,
Nature's laughter—never lacked!

Melodies Beneath the Canopy

Underneath the leafy dome,
The critters dance, make it their home.
Frogs croak their own jazzy beat,
While ants march to the rhythm of feet.

A raccoon with shades takes the stage,
Swapping tales past every age.
Hilarity blooms in every chill,
Nature's carnival—what a thrill!

Echoes in the Pinewood

Echoes bounce from tree to tree,
A chorus made of glee and glee.
Owls wink as they play peek-a-boo,
With chips and giggles from the crew.

The wind tells stories, twisty and sweet,
As the roots jiggle to the beat.
Even the sunlight joins the fun,
Playing tag till day is done!

Shadows of the Needle

Shadows dance across the floor,
While shadows of needles start to soar.
Laughter trickles like sap from bark,
In every corner, there's a spark.

A critter's prank, the punchline's quick,
Nature's glory in every flick.
With playful whispers all around,
Hilarity's the best found sound!

Dance of the Needle

In a forest where needles wiggle,
Trees break out in a silly giggle.
Branches sway to a bouncy beat,
Even the squirrels can't stay on their feet.

Pine cones drop like crazy balls,
Rolling and bouncing, ignoring the falls.
Sunny days make the needles dance,
While critters join in their merry prance.

Harmony Among the Branches

Branches gather for a grand debate,
Discussing which bird is truly great.
A jay claims he sings the best tune,
But sparrows chime in, 'You're just a buffoon!'

They settle down in a leafy brawl,
Whispering secrets to the great pine tall.
Laughter echoes through the green grove,
Making a melody that we all love.

Serenade of the Forest

In the twilight, the trees start to croon,
Frogs join in, singing with the moon.
A rabbit tap dances with a flair,
While owls hoot out a goofy prayer.

Raccoons bring snacks, setting the scene,
Chips and nuts in this forest cuisine.
Under the stars, the animals play,
Celebrating life in their funny way.

Echoes of the Tall Pines

Tall pines whisper secrets to the breeze,
Tickling the branches, making them freeze.
A gust of wind gives a cheeky shout,
As acorns tumble and giggle about.

With shadows dancing, the moon starts to beam,
Nature's chuckle sounds like a dream.
Even the fox roars with laughter bright,
In the club of the night, everything feels right.

Resonance of the Ancient Grove

In the woods where the trees play,
A squirrel danced in a funny way.
He tripped on a root,
And fell with a hoot.

The owls just laughed, they couldn't stay,
As branches swayed in a playful fray.
The breeze gave a sigh,
And so did the sky.

The acorns tossed with such delight,
They rolled and bounced, oh what a sight!
The trees whispered low,
In giggles, they glow.

A chipmunk chimed in with a rhyme,
He sang about squirrels in summertime,
In the ancient grove,
Where laughter will rove.

Soliloquy of the Rustic Thicket

In the thicket, the brambles twist,
A hedgehog pondered, feeling missed.
He searched for a friend,
But was met with a bend.

A rabbit hopped in, with a grin,
And asked if he'd like to join in.
They burrowed around,
Till they both tumbled down.

They giggled and rolled, such a pair,
With leaves in their fur, not a care.
The trees chuckled loud,
Join the jovial crowd!

The rustic charm gave them a lift,
As nature prepared for a gift.
A dance in the sun,
Where all second to none.

Overture of the Swaying Pines

The pines began to sway and hum,
Their needles jiggled to the drum.
They threw a small show,
Where the wind joined the flow.

A raccoon popped in, with a hat,
He twirled and wobbled, fancy that!
The audience cheered,
For laughter appeared.

The branches waved like they had flair,
As sunlight sparkled through the air.
A forest parade,
In merriment made.

With every sway, the laughter grew,
A symphony with a funny view.
The trees sang along,
To the jovial song.

Tales of the Twisting Trunks

Twisting trunks shared their old tales,
Of quirky critters and funny fails.
A fox that slipped,
And a bird that tripped.

They spoke of a time when the sun blazed,
And shadows danced, all amazed.
A worm in a coat,
So silly, he'd gloat.

The mushrooms giggled at the sight,
Of a beetle's dance on a moonlit night.
The trunks wrapped tight,
In the merry light.

As stars sprinkled down, the trunks sighed,
With stories old folks never denied.
In this forest of cheer,
Not a single tear.

Verses in the Verdant Wilds

In the woods where squirrels dance,
They plot with acorns in a glance.
A rabbit trips on leafy wear,
While mossy stones just sit and stare.

A bear in shades, oh what a sight,
He flexes muscles, arms held tight.
With bees that buzz in rhythmic cheer,
The forest echoes, laughter near.

Cadence of the Woodland Spirits

The whispers of the trees they tease,
As chipmunks play a game of freeze.
A raccoon dons a tiny hat,
While owls debate, 'What is that?'

With twinkling lights, the fireflies bloom,
As critters prance around the room.
A porcupine tells tales of woe,
But everyone just laughs, you know!

Symphony of the Swaying Branches

The winds compose a tune so bright,
Where branches sway and birds take flight.
A crow sings off-key, quite the show,
While bushes giggle, 'Oh, no, no!'

A fox in socks prances about,
In woodland parlors, there's no doubt.
The laughter rings through every glade,
As nature joins in the masquerade.

Aria of the Timbered Trail

Down the path where mushrooms grow,
A snail races—oh, oh, whoa!
With ferns that dance a jolly jig,
And hedgehogs join, all snug and big.

The echoes bounce from tree to tree,
As laughter flows, wild and free.
A footing slips, a tumble's grace,
In the timbered trail, it's all a race!

Chants of the Nature's Choir

In the forest, squirrels debate,
Who's the fastest at a nut raid.
Birds sing high, but who could know,
A raccoon joins in, putting on a show.

Leaves flip-flop like a dancing jig,
While hedgehogs wonder, "What is that big?"
A bear tries to waltz with grace,
But fumbles hard, what a clumsy case!

Branches sway, trying to keep beat,
While moles dig down, feeling the heat.
The wind giggles, it's having a spree,
While the pond ducks quack, "Join in with glee!"

This nature's concert, wild and grand,
Filled with laughs, not just a band.
So raise a glass, or maybe a pine,
To the hiccupping fun of the forest divine!

Rhythms of the Wintergreen

Snowflakes hover, look at them twirl,
A snowman slouches, starting to swirl.
In the whispering pines, candy canes sway,
As reindeer giggle, ruling the day.

Frosty hat tossed, where did it go?
A cheeky raccoon steals it, oh no!
Snowballs fly as laughter erupts,
The fox gets hit, as friendship erupts.

Bouncing rabbits in their winter wear,
Chasing each other without a care.
Mice take selfies,posing so neat,
While snowmen trip over their own feet!

The trees stand still, bore witness to fun,
Nature's dance, under winter's sun.
So grab a cup of cocoa, come see,
This rhythm of joy, pure glee, and spree!

Ballad of the Silent Grove

In the grove where whispers play,
A shy bear tries to join the fray.
With each step, sticks snap and crack,
He worries he'll give all the trees a whack!

Owls giggle, "Look at him try!"
While the rabbits chime in with a sigh.
The woodpecker drums, keeping the beat,
While raccoons laugh, taking a seat.

A deer attempts ballet on the grass,
But trips on roots, oh what a pass!
Squirrels mock with their bushy tails,
As the grove fills up with hilarious tales.

With pinecones rolling like clowns on a spree,
Nature's own circus, so wild and free.
Laughter erupts, echoing alike,
In this silent grove, where all delight!

Cacophony of Conifers

Pines whisper secrets, but in a jest,
"Who's the tallest? Bet you can't guess!"
While cedars chuckle, "It's not who's the best,
It's about the shade—come take a rest!"

A porcupine struts, full of grand flair,
"Stand back, everyone, I'll give you a scare!"
But instead, he tumbles, rolls down the hill,
Laughing out loud, what a funny thrill!

The wind howls softly, a tickling breeze,
Telling the cones, "Sway with such ease!"
A hedgehog slips, does a quick spin,
As laughter erupts from deep within.

This cacophony buzzes, a merry delight,
In the conifers, where joy takes flight.
So clap your paws, or wave a leafy hand,
Join the fun, it's a wild woodland band!

Whispers Among the Fir

In the forest, trees do chat,
Squirrels gossip, 'Who's that fat?'
Pinecones laugh and tumble down,
While owls swoop with sudden frown.

Branches sway, like silly dancers,
Rustling leaves are merry prancers.
Rabbits bolt, dodging the sight,
Of the sneaky fox at night.

The sun shines bright, a golden jest,
And all the critters join the fest.
The beetles march in silly lines,
Singing songs of ancient times.

Underneath the boughs they play,
Mossy floors where children stay.
Laughter bounces through the trees,
As nature chuckles in the breeze.

Phrases in a Forest Symphony

In woodlands deep, the creatures sing,
Chirping crickets make the strings.
The rabbits hop in perfect time,
While squirrels add their nutty rhyme.

Acorns drop with silly thuds,
Creating rhythms in the buds.
The bluebirds chirp a catchy tune,
As shadows dance beneath the moon.

A wise old owl gives a hoot,
Joining in the band, tooot!
Deer prance lightly, not a care,
Amid the laughter in the air.

Leaves flip pages, grass claps hands,
As nature forms the funniest bands.
Each critter knows their place in line,
In this green world, all's divine.

Rhythm of the Green Tapestry

Amidst the green, a chorus grows,
Where every bush and flower knows.
Tiny beetles tap their feet,
On a log where two frogs meet.

The wind plays pranks, a merry tease,
As branches brush and bend with ease.
Sunbeams tickle the roots below,
While giggles rise from seedlings slow.

Bees buzz beats that sound like cheer,
As flowers bloom from far and near.
A dance unfolds on nature's stage,
With every page, they share their age.

The forest's charm is wrapped in fun,
A lively place for everyone.
With each new dawn, the tales are spun,
In this green world, joy's never done.

Echoing Secrets of the Canopy

High above, the branches talk,
Secrets shared with every squawk.
A lizard's wink, a crow's deep caw,
Makes the rhythm grand, full of awe.

Leafy whispers travel far,
As fireflies join in the bizarre.
Silly shadows play tag at night,
Chasing critters in giddy flight.

The moon, a giggling friend up high,
Watches owls as they softly fly.
While lizards dance on sunlit beams,
Creating chaos in their dreams.

Beneath the trees, a joyful spree,
Raccoons laugh, a sight to see.
With every rustle and breeze that plays,
Nature's mischief brightens days.

The Essence of Sylvan Serenity

In the woods where squirrels play,
Trees gossip about their day.
Pine cones tumble with a clatter,
Leaves giggle as they scatter.

Whispers of the forest bloom,
While spiders build a cozy room.
Beneath the canopy so grand,
Squirrels dance in nature's band.

A frog jumps in a fit of glee,
Announcing that it's time for tea.
Branches swing like music bands,
Tickling tales across the lands.

Unfolding the Roots of Tradition

Roots tangled in a funny way,
Challenge every tree to play.
Around the trunk, they make a show,
Fumbling feet in nature's flow.

The owls wink with knowing grins,
As branches twist in playful spins.
What do the acorns wish to be?
Chubby champs on a tree spree!

Moss carpets all the floors so green,
Hosting parties in between.
With forest friends, they laugh and cheer,
Traditions sung from year to year.

A Serenade Beneath the Green Veil

Underneath the leafy veil,
A raccoon tells a quirky tale.
With a wink and a silly shrug,
He sneaks a snack—oh, what a thug!

The birds are crooning tunes around,
A symphony of nature's sound.
Pine needles dance with a wild swirl,
As fireflies twirl in a lively whirl.

Fungi giggle in their place,
Mushroom hats all filled with grace.
Nature calls in jovial tones,
Join the party; let's not moan!

Musings Inspired by the Timbered Sky

Looking up at the mighty trees,
Wondering who's tickled by the breeze?
A woodpecker insists he's an ace,
While windsongs put a smile on his face.

Clouds drift by, they're friendly ghosts,
Making shapes that make us boast.
"Is that a train or a giant shoe?"
The forest giggles, "That's just a view!"

Beneath branches, the shadows play,
Creating games in a bright ballet.
With laughter echoing, joys amplify,
Who knew nature could be so spry?

Eulogy of the Elderwoods

Oh, the grand old trees, reaching high,
They whisper secrets, oh my, oh my!
With bark so wrinkled, like grandpa's face,
They dance in the wind, a slow-paced race.

Squirrels hold court on branches wide,
Chattering tales of forest pride,
Acorns fall like raindrops sweet,
To the tune of thumping squirrel feet.

Mushrooms giggle beneath the shade,
In a forest party that won't soon fade,
With every breeze, a tickle and tease,
They throw wild shadows, bending knees.

So let's raise a glass to their silly sway,
These elderwoods brightening the day,
May they stand strong, with laughs in the wood,
In their goofy embrace, we all feel good.

An Ode to the Lifeblood

In the veins of trees, sap flows like wine,
A sticky elixir, oh so divine!
As bugs gather round for a sweet parade,
This nectar's the life, no plans to evade.

The woodpecker's drum beat, a silly tune,
Echoes through branches, bright as the moon,
While frogs croon loudly from their leafy lair,
Reveling in nature's wild, wacky flair.

Nature's mad circus, with vines acting sly,
Climbing and twisting, oh how they fly!
Where laughter erupts in a splash of green,
The lifeblood of woods is a comical scene.

So toast to the sap with a grin and a shout,
For all the fun that it's sprouted about,
In every drop, a giggle resides,
Let joy be the fruit that forever abides.

Resounding Quietude of the Pines

In the solitude, the pines stand tall,
Whispering secrets that ever enthrall,
Yet amidst the silence, a chuckle awakes,
As the wind plays tricks with the dead leaves' flakes.

A pinecone plops with a comedy flair,
Landing on noses like they just don't care,
With needles like fingers, they poke and tease,
Creating a ruckus in the cool, gentle breeze.

The owls hoot loudly in nocturnal jest,
Accusing the stars of a timid guest,
While shadows cavort in dappled light,
The pines giggle softly, wrapped up tight.

Here's to the pines, in their antics so fine,
Who invite us to laugh in their needle-lined shrine,
May their calmness echo with laughter so bright,
In the resounding quiet, there's joy in the night.

Reverberations Beneath the Moonlight

As the moon winks down on the forest floor,
The trees drum softly, a rhythmic score,
Bouncing giggles off branches so grand,
In a moonlit revelry, all trees take a stand.

The critters unite in a wild parade,
With shadows and moonbeams, their antics displayed,
The owls and raccoons troupe in delight,
Dancing beneath a sparkling night.

A breeze joins the fun, with a whimsical twist,
Caressing the leaves, too lovely to resist,
Whistles and chuckles mingle with the dark,
Nature's own symphony, a playful spark.

So let us celebrate under this light,
Where laughter and joy take welcome flight,
In reverberations both tender and spry,
Each moment with trees, a jubilant high.

Notes from the Misty Glade

In a glade where shadows play,
A squirrel sings in a funny way.
With acorn hats and tiny paws,
He's convinced he's the woodland's cause.

Old trees chuckle with creaky tones,
As branches sway with leafy moans.
A woodpecker dances, tapping beats,
While mushrooms wiggle on their seats.

The brook giggles, bubbling bright,
With fish that splash with sheer delight.
A hedgehog joins, a wobbly twirl,
And suddenly, the mist starts to whirl.

In this glade, humor's never shy,
As critters plan a dance-off by and by.
Between the ferns, laughter flows,
In this secret world, anything goes.

Your Heartbeat in the Shaded Wood

In the shaded wood, a rabbit spies,
With big round ears and curious eyes.
He hops along with a jaunty flair,
Chasing shadows without a care.

A butterfly flits, teasing the breeze,
While a chipmunk hums with phantom keys.
Trees sway, whispering silly tunes,
As the sun sets, revealing cartoons.

The bears below begin to dance,
With belly rolls that entertain their chance.
A deer snickers, watching the show,
Who knew the woods could have such a glow?

Your heartbeat quickens with every sound,
As laughter echoes all around.
In the shaded wood, joy takes flight,
Where every creature shares the light.

Harmonies of the Gnarled Roots

Amongst gnarled roots that twist and twine,
A raccoon croons, "This place is mine!"
With paws in the air and a wink of an eye,
He plays the roots like a banjo, oh my!

The owls hoot in rhythmic delight,
As fireflies flash like stars at night.
They buzz about, conceiving plans,
Of woodland concerts with furry bands.

A dancing frog leaps onto the stage,
Wearing spectacles and a book of age.
He reads from tales of silly yore,
While the audience giggles, demanding more.

Rooted in fun, the chorus grows,
With every tune, laughter flows.
In this woodland realm, joy resides,
Where harmony and hilarity both collide.

Tones of the Mountain's Embrace

In the mountain's embrace, echoes resound,
A goat sings opera, so wildly profound.
With a wink at the sheep, he hits a high note,
While chickens dance, in fine feathered coat.

The wind joins in with a cheeky swirl,
Tickling the trees, giving them a twirl.
A bear brings snacks, cheese and crackers,
As the critters cheer for the good-time wrackers.

From rocks and stones, the laughter flies,
As mountains grumble with laughter's sighs.
Each note is silly, each beat like a prance,
In this embrace, join the giggle dance!

The sun sets low, casting golden beams,
As snickers turn into joyful dreams.
In the mountain's tone, hilarity stakes,
A concert of joy, where silliness wakes.

Notes from the Ancient Grove

In the grove where the branches twirl,
Saplings gossip and leaves do swirl.
A squirrel plays the violin,
While the owls hoot, it's a win-win.

Mice dance in their tiny shoes,
Beneath the trees, they chase the blues.
The raccoons jam on pots and pans,
While insects hum in bands of fans.

A woodpecker taps a funny beat,
As mushrooms tap-dance on tiny feet.
The breeze laughs and teases the pines,
While acorns roll like ancient fines.

All creatures sing, in a joyful spree,
In this grove that's wild and free.
Come join the fun, don't be late,
In the grove, it's never straight!

Uplifted by the Aspens

Aspens giggle in the blustery air,
Their leaves flutter, showing off flair.
A deer in shades of dapper grace,
Stumbles upon a snail's slow race.

Chirps echo from the branches high,
As the grasshoppers leap and fly.
Frogs in tuxedos, trying to croak,
Join the dance, make the forest choke.

Bumblebees wear sunglasses cool,
Buzzing along, acting the fool.
Each twig is a stage for laughs galore,
Nature's comedy; who could ask for more?

Under the sun, they sway and spin,
In this wild dance, let's all jump in!
For every tree has a tale to tell,
In the light-hearted woods, we dwell.

Trills of the Timberland

In the timberland, tunes take flight,
Berries bounce and the owls take fright.
A moose croons a mountain song,
While squirrels giggle, dancing along.

Branches sway like they want to groove,
As shadows twist and branches move.
Every critter finds their tune,
Under the watch of the pale moon.

Raccoons steal rhythm from the night,
While fireflies twinkle, oh so bright.
The harmony sparkles, it truly shines,
As laughter rings through the pines.

Here in the wood, let the fun unfold,
With every note, a sight to behold.
In this concert, every creature plays,
In the timberland, joy's here to stay!

Serenities of the Shade

In a shady nook, where the cool winds blow,
The laughter of critters puts on quite a show.
Beneath the canopy, mischief brews,
As shadows stretch, and silliness ensues.

Chips chirp jokes that make you chuckle,
While shadows stretch, causing a shuffle.
A bear with a hat, naps on a rock,
Awakens to find his sock is a flock!

Dancing leaves make quite the parade,
As squirrels put on their finest charade.
The sunlight peeks, joining the fun,
In the shade, they shine like the sun.

So raise a glass to the forest's call,
With giggles aplenty, we have it all.
In the serene shade, laughter flows bright,
Join the revelry, until the twilight!

Chorus of the Winding Trails

In the woods, the squirrels race,
Chasing shadows, what a chase!
One leaps high, nearly slips,
He grabs a branch, while the crowd quips.

Roots like snakes twist and tangle,
We watch a dog begin to wrangle.
He finds a stick, thinks he's slick,
But trips and rolls—oh, what a trick!

The path curves back, a crafty route,
With every step, there's room for doubt.
A raccoon laughs with gleeful glee,
As we all fumble, oh, can't you see?

Giggles echo through the green,
Nature knows how to convene.
Among the trees, we trip and fall,
But laughter's loudest, after all!

Cantata of the Cool Glades

In the shade where bumblebees hum,
A frog makes sounds like a bass drum.
He croaks a tune; it's quite absurd,
Jumping on logs, like he's a bird.

The rabbits dance in a funny line,
Twisting and turning, oh how they shine!
With floppy ears, they prance around,
Then trip on roots, they hit the ground.

Nearby, a wise owl watches close,
Rolling his eyes at the silly show.
He hoots with laughter, wings spread wide,
As the forest chuckles at the wild ride.

In cool glades where mischief reigns,
The antics here soothe all our pains.
Each step brings giggles, light as a breeze,
Finding joy in moments, nature's tease!

Ballad of the Twisting Trunks

Old trees twist, their limbs do lean,
In a dance that's quite obscene.
One trunk bows down, as if to jest,
While others chuckle, feeling blessed.

Bugs on branches buzz in tune,
They've started a party beneath the moon.
Caterpillars shimmy and shake,
While beetles wonder, "Who needs a break?"

Through twisting trunks, we roam so free,
Laughing loud with friends like these.
A racquetball game with acorns fast,
Our forest fun, it's such a blast!

With each odd shape, a story blooms,
In nature's laugh, the joy resumes.
So let's kick back, embrace the muck,
For in this place, we're truly struck!

Hymn of the Great Outdoors

Beneath blue skies, we take a seat,
The ants march by with tiny feet.
They carry crumbs, their day's great feat,
While we just snack on what we eat.

A picnic spread on blankets bright,
With sandwiches, and lemonade, what a sight!
But a squirrel leaps, oh what a fright,
Stealing our lunch in a flash of light!

The tall grass waves, a friendly jest,
We see a fox in a clever quest.
He struts and poses, thinks he's the best,
But trips on roots, and we're so blessed!

In this vast wonder, laughter's the key,
We share our joys, wild and free.
With every moment and silly cheer,
The great outdoors holds loved ones near!

In the Company of Stalwart Cedars

In the woods where whispers play,
Cedars jest beneath the day.
Squirrels giggle, tails held high,
Trees chuckle, reaching for the sky.

Branches dance with leafy cheer,
Breezes carry laughter near.
A fox hops in, slips on a cone,
The splat gives him a brand-new tone.

A woodpecker taps out a tune,
Echoing laughter beneath the moon.
Old Cedars creak with jesting grace,
In this goofy, leafy place.

Beneath the shade, stories are spun,
Nature's comedy, all in good fun!
Chirping birds on branches swing,
Together they make the forest sing.

The Tryst of Earthly Creatures and Boughs

Critters gather for a chat,
A hedgehog rolls, a cat sits flat.
Boughs above play hide and seek,
Squeaks and chuckles, what a peak!

A rabbit hops on soft green grass,
Nearby, a turtle moves with sass.
"What's for lunch?" the rabbit asks,
The turtle grins, says, "Let's task!"

Boughs sway gently, gossiping bright,
Sharing secrets, pure delight.
In this tryst of silly friends,
Laughter flows, and time transcends.

So they feast on berries sweet,
Under shadows, a cozy seat.
As dusk descends, they start to snore,
In their world, there's always more!

Blossoms in the Thickening Aroma

Blossoms burst in vibrant hues,
Petals dance, it's good news!
The fragrance flirts with buzzing bees,
A floral party in the breeze.

A ladybug sips nectar fine,
While ants march by, they're feeling fine.
Every bloom has stories to tell,
Amongst the scents, they cast their spell.

Silly butterflies flit and swirl,
Trying to impress a shy squirrel.
The forest giggles, hears the buzz,
In this thriving land, who cares what was?

As day slips into evening's hug,
Creatures snuggle, feel the tug.
With laughter and joy their hearts grow,
In this fragrant, playful show.

The Brightness Within Shadowed Loams

Underneath where shadows play,
Bright little critters come to sway.
Worms wiggle in a merry band,
While mushrooms pop up, bold and grand.

A hedgehog rolls, a beetle slides,
Sneaky moles play games that bide.
Rich loam whispers secrets low,
While laughter bubbles, life in flow.

Roots tangle, sharing tales of yore,
Fungi giggle, wanting more.
They chuckle while the world above,
For here they find their joy, their love.

As the night wraps all in grace,
Creatures' jokes fill every space.
In hidden land, where shadows bloom,
There's light and laughter in every room.

The Quiet Cacophony Within

In the forest, trees chat
About the squirrels and their acrobat
A dance of branches, tangled limbs,
While owls laugh at their silly whims.

The pinecones drop, a little prank,
Each thud a giggle, the trees all flank.
The ferns whisper secrets, you won't believe,
As raccoons waltz under the quiet eaves.

Branches sway like they're in a show,
A forest dance-off, put on a glow.
Critters throw shade, and ferns throw sass,
Laughter rustles across the grass.

So come join the evergreen jest,
Where life's a jape and humor's blessed.
Nature's comic, no need for a script,
In this green laughter, all are equipped.

Immortal Whispers in the Wind

The wind carries tales from the heights,
Of giggling leaves and quiet frights.
A dandelion puff, a fleeting sight,
Tickles your nose, then takes flight.

Breezes chuckle, pushing pine,
Every twist a punchline, so divine.
They whisper secrets, ancient lore,
Of trees that joke, forevermore.

A gust whooshes, a squirrel shouts,
Dodging branches, dancing about.
Laughter rustles through green attire,
Even the moss has the urge to inspire.

So listen close to the playful breeze,
Tickling fingers and bustling leaves.
In the depths of silence, humor rings,
Nature's chorus, in jest, it sings.

Tranquil Tones of the Thicket

In the thicket, where shadows play,
Branches gossip in a fun-filled way.
The bushes blush with every word,
As giggles echo, silly and stirred.

A beetle rolls a leaf, quite proud,
While crickets chirp, a raucous crowd.
The saplings sway, a comical sprout,
Tickled by laughter, there's no doubt.

A fox shrugs at a riddle played,
"Why did the tree bring a cascade?"
Nature chuckles in rhythmic tune,
Under the watch of the grinning moon.

So come, let's dwell in this jovial glade,
With nature's humor, never afraid.
In the quiet thicket, silliness reigns,
Life springs forth where laughter gains.

Sweet Sustenance of the Sprites

Tiny sprites with mischievous grins,
Share tales of acorns and berry skins.
They sprinkle honey on the tree's bark,
And tickle the night with their cheeky spark.

A brook babbles jokes to the stones,
While frogs croak songs in funny tones.
Stars stutter laughter, twinkling bright,
In the sprinkle of dew, a pure delight.

Mushrooms smirk, huddled in glee,
They swap stories with the slumbering bee.
With every twist, the forest blooms,
In this jolly realm, humor consumes.

So raise a toast with wildflower wine,
To the sprites who make the woods divine.
Where laughter grows and sweetness thrives,
In every nook, the joy survives.

Melodic Breath of the Wilderness

In the woods, a squirrel danced,
A bird named Chucklet cheered his chance.
They twirled and spun, with goofy glee,
Nature's joy is wild and free.

Trees wore hats made of shiny leaves,
Whispering secrets to the evening breeze.
A raccoon juggled acorns with flair,
The forest chuckled, what a rare affair!

A bear in shades took a lazy snooze,
Played guitar, announced the good news.
With every strum, the critters clapped,
Such a bash beneath the trees they mapped.

So when you stroll through this green parade,
Remember the mischief and the masquerade.
For nature sings with a comical twist,
In every shadow, a joke exists.

The Tranquil Heart of Trees

Beneath the oak, a fox wore shoes,
He pranced about, with silly moves.
The trees all hummed a happy tune,
As fireflies flickered, up to the moon.

A wise old owl quipped, "What's the fuss?
This is where we find our trust!"
The rabbits giggled, hiding near,
In the heart of the forest, there's nothing to fear.

Leaves played cards, oh what a sight,
Branching out through day and night.
The wind blew whispers, "Let's have some fun!"
Every creature joined in, one by one.

So wander slowly, take your time,
Embrace the humor, feel the rhyme.
In the tranquil heart where laughter grows,
A world of wonders, anything goes.

The Green Guardians' Anthem

In the tall pines, a party's begun,
A beetle DJ spins, oh what fun!
The mushrooms bobbed, like they're at a fair,
While chipmunks cut a rug without a care.

"Hey there, Woody!" called out a lark,
"Let's jazz it up, we'll leave a mark!"
The trees clapped along to the beetle's beat,
With roots tapping rhythms, oh what a treat!

Badgers cheered, with snacks to share,
"Grab a twig, let down your hair!"
The stars peeked in, took a little glance,
And frolicked quietly, joining the dance.

From dawn to dusk, they embraced the day,
In joyful cheer, they kept worries at bay.
As laughter echoed, the forest spun,
In the heart of green, there's always fun.

Nature's Vigil in the Glen

At dawn, the critters gathered tight,
For a giggle-fest of pure delight.
A porcupine wore a wild pink tie,
While raccoons plotted pranks nearby.

A turtle pondered, "What's next for me?"
"Let's build a castle, just wait and see!"
The hedgehog grinned, with a wink in his eye,
As squirrels zipped by, oh my, oh my!

With twigs for wands, they cast out spells,
While butterflies hummed their playful bells.
The brook giggled softly, as it skipped along,
In nature's vigil, it's a merry song.

So if you're down, take a joyful trip,
To the glen of glee, let your worries slip.
For laughter's a treasure, oh can you tell?
In the heart of the wild, all is well!

Veneration of the Verdant Reach

In the forest, trees do sway,
Singing to the sun all day.
Squirrels dance and chitter cheer,
While pine cones drop, what a queer.

Woodpeckers tap their funny beat,
As beetles march on tiny feet.
Branches wave, they take a bow,
Nature's jest, so funny now.

The moss is soft, a velvet floor,
While critters play, we all adore.
A deer trips over roots, oh dear!
Laughter whispers, can you hear?

With leaves that giggle, rustling light,
Trees act silly, bringing delight.
In every crack and leafy groove,
The verdant realm knows how to move.

Heartbeat of the Timbered Realm

The woods alive, a lively show,
Tree trunks dance, they steal the glow.
Frogs in croaks, make merry sounds,
Jumping squirrels, round and round.

A rabbit joins the wobbly jam,
It hops along, with a little slam.
The owls hoot, they crack a grin,
In this realm, fun's never thin.

Clouds float by; they've grown some feet,
Trees tickle them as they meet.
Giggles echo from limb to limb,
Nature's joy, never dim.

Sunshine sprinkles laughter wide,
In the timber, antics collide.
Nature's heart keeps pumping fun,
In the shade, all creatures run.

The Oath of the Evergreen Guardians

The guardians stand, with a playful wink,
Pine needles drop; they never think.
Guarding all with roots so strong,
Even when the day feels wrong.

Saplings stretch with silly glee,
Tickling creatures, come and see!
The laughter rings from tree to tree,
Whispered secrets, wild and free.

A windy day plays tricks like mad,
Shaking branches, it's all so glad.
They stand their ground, refuse to pout,
Evergreens wear fun like a shout.

In the twilight, shadows dance,
The guardians twirl in a leafy trance.
Every crack is filled with cheer,
Together we laugh, all are near.

Convergence of Earth and Sky

When earth and sky begin to play,
Clouds giggle, in bright array.
The trees bend low to hear the joke,
With every breeze, the laughter stroke.

Birds swoop down, they dive and dart,
Their chirps compose a merry part.
In tandem, branches twist with flair,
Yet roots stay firm, without a care.

Rain drops fall with a cheeky grin,
Each puddle forms a splash within.
The world alive, a valiant cheer,
Nature's music—a joy, so near.

Winds whisper tales of silly heights,
Convergence leads to giggly sights.
Beneath this grand, enchanted sky,
The earth and trees all laugh and sigh.

Harmony of the Forest Heart

The trees wear suits of green and brown,
With branches that sway in a leafy gown.
They whisper jokes to the passing breeze,
While squirrels plan parties with acorn keys.

The owls hoot laughter, perched up high,
Mocking the deer that stumble by.
The roots all dance in the cool, damp ground,
As mushrooms giggle, their caps all around.

In this woodland, all creatures cheer,
For every laugh draws friends near.
The sun draws smiles from leaves up high,
As shadows play hide and seek by and by.

So join the fun, in nature's choir,
Where laughter's the tune and joy won't tire.
From tiny ants to the tall, proud pine,
This forest heart sings, oh so fine!

Serenade of the Tallest Trees

The tallest trees reach for the sky,
Bragging to clouds that float on by.
They twirl and twist in a gentle breeze,
While gophers below wear snazzy sleeves.

The woodpecker drums with a cheeky smile,
As critters gather, stay for a while.
Caterpillars groove on a leafy stage,
While fireflies dance, all the rage.

A conifer sneezes, the pines all roar,
They laugh so hard, who could want more?
With echoes of joy ringing so clear,
Every woodland spirit draws near.

So sway with the trees, join in the jest,
For nature's chorus is simply the best.
With branches entwined, let laughter burst,
In this forest of fun, we're never dispersed!

Lullabies of the Forest Floor

Down on the forest floor so lush,
Where mushrooms peek with a quiet hush.
They tell sweet tales to the drowsy bees,
As crickets play tunes on their knees.

Frogs croak softly, a nighttime show,
Their rhythm's a giggle, oh what a flow!
The starlit sky winks down with glee,
Hoping to catch a joke or three.

The tiny ants march a funny parade,
With candy crumbs they've cheerfully made.
As twigs tap dance in the glow of the moon,
Even the shadows hum a silly tune.

So snuggle in close, let laughter soar,
These lullabies are never a chore.
In the cradle of nature, dreams take flight,
As the forest whispers, "Good night, good night."

Breezes Through the Boughs

The breezes swirl through branches wide,
Tickling leaves as they glide and slide.
The whispering wind tells tales so funny,
Of bashful blooms and bees all sunny.

With a puff and a whoosh, the trees play tag,
While raccoons chuckle, and hedgehogs wag.
The soft rustle spreads giggles around,
As flowers laugh at the sights they've found.

The breeze then tickles the noses of deer,
They jump and prance, oh my, oh dear!
The hazel bushes sway in delight,
While fireflies flash, lighting up the night.

So let the breezes carry your cheer,
With each gust of giggles, let's spread it here.
In the playful winds, let your heart be free,
Join nature's jest, wild and carefree!

The Secret Language of Saplings

Little trees whisper tales of the breeze,
Asking squirrels to join in their tease.
A conifer giggles, swaying in the sun,
While beetles on branches just want some fun.

Mossy hats perched on each tiny head,
Dancing with joy as the sunlight is spread.
In this woodland chatter, no secret is lost,
Except maybe who really ate the last frost.

Saplings in a circle, sharing their dreams,
Plotting to outgrow the tallest of beams.
"Let's stretch up and tickle the clouds!" they declare,
While ants march in rhythms, quite unaware.

So next time you wander, take time to listen,
To leafy convos that sparkle and glisten.
You might find a secret or two in a laugh,
As trees plot their schemes, like a wild-crafted staff.

Memories in the Mossed Earth

In dampened corners where shadows take hold,
Mossy green carpets with stories untold.
A rabbit named Rufus, with dreams of his own,
Thinks the grass whispers sweet, "You're never alone!"

Stones tell of picknicks, a loaf left to mold,
While worms tell the tales of the secrets they hold.
Old roots remind us of times gone by,
When beetles would dance as the stars painted sky.

Tufts of bright clover play games of their own,
While gophers just laugh at the fuss they have grown.
"Why not just chill under layers of dew?
No one can catch us! Not even a shoe!"

So the memories flourish in earth's soft embrace,
With whispers of laughter that time can't erase.
Invite in the antics, let worries disperse,
In mossed earth's haven, each day's a good verse.

Fragrance of Forgotten Days

A scent in the air that tickles the nose,
Of pinecones and laughter, where silliness flows.
The daydreaming flowers gossip in bloom,
As bees share their secrets with playful perfume.

On branches that wiggle, squirrels scurry and twirl,
Behind leafy curtains, their muddy paws swirl.
Each sniff brings a chuckle from what once was new,
As sunlight breaks through with a glimmering view.

Old stumps hold wisdom like grandpas in chairs,
Telling tall tales of their past woodland flares.
With giggles of saplings, all spry and full glee,
They plot pranks on tired old trees by the sea.

So join in this frolic, take a deep breath,
Let fragrances guide you, forget all the rest.
The memories dance in the sun-kissed array,
Where laughter becomes the light of the day.

Quietude Among the Pines

In a quiet glade where the tall pines sway,
Laughter erupts in the most unexpected way.
A crow with a hat, trying hard to look cool,
Suits the antics by the wise old school.

Branches stretch wide, a stage for the show,
As owls hoot along, stealing moments of glow.
A chorus of crickets, with pines as their mics,
Sing out their wisdom, as day softly hikes.

The shadows grow longer, the giggles grow too,
As saplings recall a mischief or two.
"Let's climb up the trunk and shout out to space!
Maybe we'll tickle a cloud in the race!"

So amid the tranquility, laughter unfolds,
Among the tall pines, every secret is bold.
A world of merriment lies in their sway,
In this quietude, joy finds its way.

The Embrace of the Woodland Spirits

In the forest, trees do dance,
With branches swaying, quite a prance.
Squirrels giggle, cheeky and spry,
While seeing who can leap the highest to the sky.

Moss carpets the ground with a soft cheer,
While gnomes are whispering, lend me your ear.
A deer in a tutu strikes a bold pose,
And raccoons plot mischief, who knows where it goes!

A rabbit plays trumpet, so grand and so loud,
The flowers all sway, oh, they're feeling proud.
The owls are laughing, what quite a scene,
A ballet of nature, all dressed in green!

So if you wander beneath leafy boughs,
Prepare for a show, take a bow, take a bow!
For woodland spirits will sprinkle delight,
In this comical stage, both day and by night.

Interwoven Lives of Leaf and Light

Sunlight jiggles through leaf and vine,
As ants throw a party, all dressed to shine.
A chipmunk in shades struts down a trail,
While butterflies gossip, each tale a detail.

The wind sings a tune, it's slightly off-key,
It tickles the leaves, now that's amusing to see!
A playful raccoon steals berries with flair,
Dressed in a mask, like a woodland fair!

Bees buzzing happy, a concert in bloom,
They've formed a new band, with flowers for room.
The beetles tap rhythms, a snazzy parade,
As trees sway and sway, in this grand masquerade!

It's a life made of laughter, where all seem so bright,
A tapestry woven with joy and delight.
Come join the frolic, let's dance and unite,
In this woodland ball under soft, sparkling light.

Ancestral Echoes in the Grove

In the grove where shadows softly creep,
Whispers of ancestors gently leap.
A wise old owl hoots, perched on a beam,
While squirrels munch calmly, plotting a dream.

A fox in a cloak speaks of ancient lore,
Of tasty acorns and nuts galore.
The trees nod along, with a rustling cheer,
As echoes of laughter draw ever so near.

Ghostly raccoons are hosting a roast,
Telling tall tales of the ones they love most.
The echoes ring out with hysterical flair,
While shadows dance wildly, without a care.

So gather around for a night full of cheer,
With laughter and stories for all who are here.
In this magical grove where history flows,
Underneath starry skies, where hilarity grows.

Tones of Resilience Carried on the Breeze

The wind is a joker, it tickles the pines,
With grizzly bears grinning as sunshine reclines.
While trees hold their ground, roots deep in the muck,
And play games of tag with the passing luck.

The bumblebees buzz with a cheeky jest,
Finding nectar as sweet as a very fine fest.
Tiny turtles giggle, racing the breeze,
With laughter and joy that will put you at ease.

Clouds float like marshmallows, fluffy and white,
With hints of a storm that tickle the night.
While nature herself, in her whimsical ways,
Brings tones of resilience, brightening our days.

So take a deep breath, soak in the cheer,
As whispers of fun tickle your ear.
In this land of wonder, where silliness rules,
Look to the trees, for they are the jewels!

Carols of the High Canopy

In the treetops, squirrels prance,
They dance and twirl, they take a chance.
With acorns flying all around,
Laughter echoes through the ground.

A bluebird sings a silly tune,
While raccoons argue, none too soon.
They tumble down from branch to branch,
All in a frenzy, what a branch!

The leaves all chuckle, green with glee,
As critters host their jubilee.
They twirl and spin, a furry crowd,
In the trees, they laugh out loud.

So if you wander through the woods,
Just listen close, feel the moods.
Nature's concert, a comical sight,
With every chirp, the day feels bright.

Songs of the Hollowed Hearts

A woodpecker pecks with great delight,
His rhythm makes the forest bright.
The rabbits hopping in a race,
Stop to ponder with a funny face.

The owls hoot with a wise old jest,
While deer prance in their Sunday best.
A bear steals honey, what a mess!
Sticky paws mean playful stress!

The brook babbles with a giggle or two,
As frogs leap high, on cue, on cue!
The fireflies blink with mischief at night,
Winking as they dance in the moonlight.

So join the fun, be part of the glee,
In every nook and cranny, take a spree.
Nature's humor, a winding path,
Brings smiles and chuckles, oh what a laugh!

Reverie of the Verdant Heights

The tallest trees wear hats of green,
They sway and jiggle, what a scene!
With branches waving, they declare,
   A parade of fun is in the air!

The chipmunks chatter, full of cheer,
As they share secrets, loud and clear.
   One tips his hat, and off they fly,
Chasing shadows beneath the sky.

A squirrel slipped on a dewy leaf,
And tumbled down, oh, such belief!
With furry friends, they rolled in glee,
   Giggling echoes in the trees.

Through dappled light, the laughter flows,
   Wherever you look, a comic show.
In leafy realms where joy collides,
   A reverie of life abides.

Chords of the Rocking Boughs

The branches sway, a rocking band,
With birds that play, the best they can.
A parrot squawks, a silly note,
While squirrels compete to stay afloat.

Down below, a hedgehog spins,
He rolls right into a patch of pins.
With prickles laughing, they form a crew,
While beetles march in shiny shoes.

A tandem of owls, wise and bright,
Swap jokes under the pale moonlight.
Their hoots blend in with rustling leaves,
Creating tunes that no one believes!

So grab a friend, come hear the sounds,
The chords of nature, joy abounds.
In every nook, a giggle grows,
Among the trees, fun overflows.

www.ingramcontent.com/pod-product-compliance
Lightning Source LLC
Chambersburg PA
CBHW051634160426
43209CB00004B/641